ECHOES OF THE ORIENT

THEOSOPHICAL DOCTRINES

First Edition 1890
William Q Judge

New Edition 2019
Edited by Tarl Warwick

COPYRIGHT AND DISCLAIMER

FOREWORD

The following booklet is one of the foremost and most well known works within the corpus of literature of Theosophy. Written at the end of the 19th century by none other than William Judge, who was acting VP of the Theosophical movement at the time, it expresses the basic views of the philosophy prior to its height of dominance, which came a decade later. Inspired largely by Blavatsky, Theosophy was more than a club or basic order and became a fairly powerful force within spiritual and especially polite society.

The lore here is largely Hindu in derivation, speaking of the concept of the Mahatma (adapted into the Theosophical idea of the adept), Devachan (a sort of long lasting paradise between physical incarnations) and much more. While not all of the adapted religious lore was always in its most authentic state, Theosophy did, for the first time, record, study, and promulgate much of that material to the West- and some of the philosophy then derided has found acceptance, especially with regards to the form of the universe and the dating of the Earth.

This edition of "Echoes of the Orient" has been edited for word usage and format. Care has been taken to retain all original intent and meaning.

ECHOES OF THE ORIENT

Dedicated To:

Helena Petrovna Blavatsky

With Love and

Gratitude by the Author

ECHOES OF THE ORIENT

ANTECEDENT WORDS

The title for these articles was chosen by Miss Kate Field when they were first sent for publication in her new paper, Kate Field's Washington, in January, 1890, and to her belongs all the credit for an appropriate name. The use of the nom de plume 'Occultus' was also the suggestion of Miss Field, since it was intended that the personality of the author should be hidden until the series was completed.

The restrictions upon the treatment of the subject growing out of the popular character of the paper in which they were published precluded the detail and elaboration that would have been possible in a philosophical or religious periodical. No pretense is made that the subject of Theosophy as understood in the Orient has been exhaustively treated, for, believing that millions of years have been devoted by the sages who are the guardians of Theosophical truth to its investigation, I think no one writer could do more than to repeat some of the echoes reaching his ears.

William Q. Judge.
New York, September, 1890.

ECHOES FROM THE ORIENT

I

What appears to the Western mind to be a very strange superstition prevails in India about wonderful persons who are said to be of immense age, and who keep themselves secluded in places not accessible to the ordinary traveler. So long has this been current in India that the name applied to these beings is well known in the Sanskrit language: 'Mahatma,' a compound of two words, maha- great, and atma- soul. The belief in the existence of such persons is not confined to the ignorant, but is shared by the educated of all castes. The lower classes look upon the Mahatmas as a sort of gods, and think most of their wonderful powers and great age. The pundits, or learned class, and educated Hindus in general, have a different view ; they say that Mahatmas are men or souls with unlimited knowledge of natural laws and of man's history and development.

They claim also that the Mahatmas- or Rishees, as they sometimes call them- have preserved the knowledge of all natural laws for ages, not only by tradition among their disciples, but also by actual records and in libraries existing somewhere in the many underground temples and passages in India. Some believers assert that there are also stores of books and records in secluded parts all over that part of Tibet which is not known to Europeans, access to them being possible only for the Mahatmas and Adepts. The credence given to such a universal theory grows out of an old Indian doctrine that man is a Spiritual being- a soul, in other words- and that this soul takes on different bodies from life to life on earth in order at last to arrive at such perfect knowledge, through repeated experience, as to enable one to assume a body fit to be the dwelling-place of a Mahatma or perfected soul. Then, they say, that particular soul becomes a spiritual helper to mankind. The perfected men are said to know the truth about the genesis of worlds and systems, as well as the development of man upon this and other planets. Were such doctrines held only in India, it would be natural to pass the subject by with this brief mention.

But when it is found that a large body of people in America and Europe hold the same beliefs, it is interesting to note such an un-Western development of thought. The Theosophical Society was founded in New York in 1875, with the avowed object of forming a nucleus for a Universal Brotherhood, and its founders state that they believe the Indian Mahatmas directed them to establish such a society. Since its foundation it has gained members in all countries, including people of wealth as well as those in moderate circumstances, and the highly cultured also. Within its ranks there flourish beliefs in the Mahatmas of India and in Reincarnation and its twin doctrine, Karma. This last holds that no power, human or divine, can save one from the consequences of acts performed, and that in this life we are experiencing the results due to us for all acts and thoughts which were ours in the preceding incarnation. This has brought out a large body of literature in books and magazines published in the United States, England, India, and elsewhere. Newspapers are published in the interest of the new-old cult in the vernacular of Hindistan and also in old Ceylon. Even Japan has its periodicals devoted to the same end, and to ignore so wide-spread a movement would bespeak ignorance of the factors at work in our development.

When such an eminent authority as the great French savant, Emile Bournouf, says that the Theosophical movement must be counted as one of the three great religious influences in the world today, there is no need of an excuse for presenting its features in detail to readers imbued with the civilization of the West.

II

In my former paper I merely hinted at the two principal doctrines promulgated by the Theosophical Society; it is well now to notice the fact that the Society itself was organized amid a shout of laughter, which at intervals ever since has been repeated. Very soon after it launched forth, its president. Col. H. S. Olcott, who during our late war was a familiar figure in Washington, found a new member in Baron Henry Louis de Palm, who died and obligingly left his body to the Colonel to be cremated. The funeral was held at Masonic Hall, New York, and attracted great attention. It was Theosophical in its character. Col. Olcott presided, a Spiritualist offered an invocation, and a Materialist read a service. All this, of course, drew forth satire from the press, but served the purpose of gaining some attention for the young Society. Its history since then has been remarkable, and it is safe to say that no other similar body in this century has drawn to itself so much consideration, stirred up such a thinking among people on mystical subjects, and grown so rapidly amid the loudest derision and against the fiercest opposition, within the short space of fifteen years.

While the press has been sneering and enemies have been plotting, the workers in the Society have established centers all over the world, and are to-day engaged persistently in sending out Theosophical literature into every nook and comer of the United States. A glance at the Theosophical map shows a line of Branches of the Society dotting a strip of this country which reaches from the city of New York to the Pacific Coast; at either end this belt spreads out to take in Boston and New Orleans in the East and San Francisco and San Diego in the West; while near the middle of the continent there is another accumulation of centers. This is claimed to be strictly and mystically Theosophical, because at each end of the magic line of effort and at its central point their is an accumulation of nuclei. It is a fact that the branches of the Society in America are rapidly running up into the first hundred. For some little time there existed in Washington a Branch of the Society called the Gnostic, but it never engaged in any active work. After it had been once incontinently dissolved by its president, who thereafter withdrew, leaving the presidency in the hands of another, the governing body of the American Theosophists formally dischartered the Gnostic, and its members joined other Branches. There is, however, today a, Washington Branch named boldly after the much lauded and belittled Mme. H. P. Blavatsky, while the Theosophical map shows an accumulation of influences in Washington that point to an additional Branch, and inquiry in official quarters discloses the fact that the matter is already mooted.

The Theosophical map of which I have spoken is a curiosity, an anomaly in the nineteenth century. Few of the members are allowed to see it; but those who are say that it is a register of the actual state, day by day, of the whole United States Section- a sort of weather map, with areas of pressure and Theosophical humidity in all directions. Where a Branch is well founded and in good condition, the spot or sensitive surface shows clearness and fixity. In certain places which are in a formative condition there is another appearance symptomatic of a vortex that may soon bring forth a Branch; while, wherever the principle of disintegration has crept into an existing organization, there the formerly bright and fixed spots grow cloudy. By means of this map, those who are managing the real growth of the movement can tell how it is going and aid it intelligently. Of course all this sounds ridiculous in our age; but, whether true or false, there are many Theosophists who believe it. A similar arrangement would be desirable in other branches of our civilization.

ECHOES OF THE ORIENT

The grand theories of the Theosophists regarding evolution, human races, religions and general civilization, as well as the future state of man and the various planets he inhabits, should engage our more serious attention; and of these I propose to speak at another time.

III

The first Echo from the burnished and mysterious East which reverberated from these pages sounded the note of Universal Brotherhood. Among the men of this day such an idea is generally accepted as vague and Utopian, but one which it will do no harm to subscribe to; they therefore quickly assent, and as quickly nullify the profession by action in the opposite direction. For the civilization of today, and especially of the United States, is an attempt to accentuate and glorify the individual. The oft-repeated declaration that any born citizen may aspire to occupy the highest office in the gift of the nation is proof of this, and the Mahatmas who guard the truth through the ages while nations are decaying, assert that the re-action is sure to come in a relapse into the worst forms of anarchy. The only way to prevent such a relapse is for men to really practice the Universal Brotherhood they are willing to accept with the tongue.

These exalted beings further say that all men are- as a scientific and dynamic fact- united, whether they admit it or not; and that each nation suffers, on the moral as well as the physical plane, from the faults of all other nations, and receives benefit from the others also even against its will. This is due to the existence of an imponderable, tenuous medium which interpenetrates the entire globe, and in which all the acts and thoughts of every man are felt and impressed, to be afterward reflected again. Hence, say the Adepts, the thoughts or the doctrines and beliefs of men are of the higher importance, because those that prevail among people of a low character are just as much and as easily reflected upon the earth as are the thoughts and beliefs of persons occupying a higher plane of culture. This is a most important tenet, if true; for, with the aid of the discoveries just now admitted by science respecting hypnotism, we are at once able to see that an enormous hypnotizing machine is about. As this tenuous medium- called by the men of the East 'Akasa' and by the medieval philosophers the 'Astral Light'- is entirely beyond our control, we are at the mercy of the pictures made in it and reflected upon us.

If to this we add the wonderfully interesting doctrine of Reincarnation, remembering also that the images made in the Astral Light persist for centuries, it is at once seen that upon returning again to earth life we are affected for good or evil by the conduct, the doctrine and the aspirations of preceding nations and men. Returning here now, for instance, we are moved, without our knowledge, by the impressions made in the Astral Light at the time when the Indians, the Spaniards and the harsh Puritans lived upon the earth. The words of the immortal Shakespeare...

"The evil that men do lives after them;
The good is oft interred with their bones,"

...receive a striking exemplification under this doctrine. For, as the evil thoughts and deeds are the more material and therefore more firmly impacted into the Astral Light, while the good, being spiritual, easily fade out, we are in effect at the mercy of the evil done. And the Adepts assert that Shakespeare was, unconsciously to himself, inspired by one of their own number. I shall refer again to this branch of the subject. The scheme of evolution put forth by these beings and their disciples is so broad, deep and far reaching as to stagger the ordinary mind. It takes in with ease periods of years running up into trillions and quadrillions. It claims that man has been on earth for millions of years more than science yet is willing to admit. It is not bound by the narrow scheme of biblical chronologists, nor startled by the magnificent age of civilizations which disappeared long ago. The keepers of this doctrine say that they and their predecessors lived in those older times, and have preserved not only the memory of them, but also complete records. These records, moreover, are not merely on perishable paper and palm leaf, but on imperishable stone. They point to such remains as the statues twenty-seven feet high found on Easter Island; to rows of gigantic statues in Asia, that by their varying heights show the gradual diminution of human stature, which kept pace with other degenerations; and, to crown all, they say that they possess today in the East the immense and well guarded collections of records of all sorts. Not only are these records said to relate to the physical history of man, but also to his astral and spiritual evolution.

Before closing this paper, I can only indicate one of their basic doctrines in the scheme of evolution. That is, that the evolution of the inner, astral form of man came first in order, and continued for an immense number of years before his physical structure was built up around it. This, with other portions of the doctrine, is vital and w411 aid much in an understanding of the complex questions presented to us by the history of the human race, both that which is known and that which is still resting on conjecture.

IV

The records to which in my last paper I referred, as having been kept by the Adepts and now in the possession of their present representatives and successors- Adepts also- relate not only to the birth of planets in this solar system, but also to the evolution and development of man, through the various kingdoms of nature, until he reaches the most perfect condition which can be imagined. The evolution of the human being includes not only the genesis of his mortal frame, but, as well, the history of the inner man, whom they are accustomed to call the real one. This, then, brings us to a very interesting claim put forward for the Wisdom Religion, that it pretends to throw light not only upon man's emotions and mental faculties, but also upon his pre-natal and post-mortem states, both of which are of the highest interest and importance. Such questions as, 'Where have I come from?' and, 'What shall be my condition after death?' trouble and confuse the minds of all men, ignorant or cultured. Priests and thinkers have, from time to time, formulated theories, more or less absurd, as to those pre-natal and post-mortem states, while the Science of today laughs in derision at the idea of making any inquiry into the matter whatever.

Theologians have offered explanations, all of which relate only to what they suppose will happen to us after death, leaving entirely out of view and wholly unanswered the natural question, 'What were we before we were born here?' And, taking them on their own ground, they are in a most illogical position, because, having once postulated immortality for the soul- the real man- they cannot deny immortality in either direction. If man is immortal, that immortality could never have had a beginning, or else it would have an end. Hence their only escape from the dilemma is to declare that each soul is a special creation. But this doctrine of a special creation for each soul born upon the earth, is not dwelt upon or expounded by the priests, inasmuch as it is deemed better to keep it discreetly in the background.

The Wisdom Religion, on the other hand, remains logical from beginning to end. It declares that man is a spiritual being, and allows of no break in the chain of anything once declared immortal. The Ego of each man is immortal; 'always was existent, always will be, and never can be nonexistent;'

appearing now and again, and reappearing, clothed in bodies on each occasion different, it only appears to be mortal; it always remains the substratum and support for the personality acting upon the stage of life. And in those appearances as mortal, the questions mooted above- as to the prenatal and post-mortem states- are of vital interest, because knowledge or ignorance concerning them alters man's thought and action while an actor on the stage, and it is necessary for him to know in order that he may so live as to aid in the grand upward sweep of the evolutionary wave.

Now the Adepts have for ages pursued scientific experimentation and investigation upon those lines. Seers themselves of the highest order, they have recorded not only their own actual experiences beyond the veil of matter, on both sides, but have collected, compared, analyzed and preserved the records of experiences of the same sort by hundreds of thousands of lesser seers, their own disciples; and this process has been going on from time immemorial. Let Science laugh as it may, the Adepts are the only true scientists, for they take into account every factor in the question, whereas Science is limited by brain-power, by circumstance, by imperfection of instruments, and by a total inability to perceive anything- deeper than the mere phenomena presented by matter. The records of the visions and experiences of the greater and lesser seers, through the ages, are extant today. Of their mass, nothing has been accepted except that which has been checked and verified by millions of independent observations; and therefore the Adepts stand in the position of those who possess actual experimental knowledge of what precedes the birth of the Ego in a human form, and what succeeds when the 'mortal coil' is cast away.

This recording of experiences still goes on, for the infinity of the changes of Nature in its evolution permits of no stoppage, no 'last word,' no final declaration. As the earth sweeps around the sun, it not only passes through new places in its orbit, but, dragged as it is by the sun through his greater orbit, involving millions of millions of years, it must in that larger circle enter upon new fields in space and unprecedented conditions. Hence the Adepts go farther yet and state that, as the phenomena presented by matter today are different from those presented a| million years ago, so matter will in another million of years show different phenomena still. Indeed, if we could translate our sight to that time, far back in the past of our globe, we could see conditions and phenomena of the material world so different from those now surrounding us that it would be almost impossible to believe we had ever been in such a state as that then prevailing. And the changes toward the conditions that will prevail at a point equally remote in advance of us, in time, and which will be not less than those that have occurred, are in progress now. Nothing in the material world endures absolutely unchanged in itself or its conditions, even for the smallest conceivable portion of time.

All that is, is forever in process of becoming something else. This is not mere transcendentalism, but is an old established doctrine called, in the East, 'the doctrine of the constant, eternal change of atoms from one state into another.'

V

The ancient doctrine of the constant, eternal change of every atom from state to state, is founded upon, or rather grows out of, another which postulates that there is no such thing as dead matter. At every conceivable point in the universe there are lives; nowhere can be found a spot that is dead; and each life is forever hastening onward to higher evolution. To admit this, we must of course grant that matter is never perceived by the eye or through any instrument. It is but the phenomena of matter that we recognize with the senses, and hence, say the sages, the thing denominated 'matter' by us is an illusion. Even the protoplasm of the schools is not the original matter; it is simply another of the phenomena.

This first original matter is called by Paracelsus and others primordial matter, the nearest approach to which in the Eastern school is found in the Sanskrit word mulaprakriti. This is the root of matter, invisible, not to be weighed, or measured, or tested with any instrument of human invention. And yet it is the only real matter underlying all the phenomena to which we erroneously give its name. But even it is not dead, but full of the lives first referred to.

Now, bearing this in mind, we consider the vast solar system, yet vast only when not compared with the still greater aggregation of stars and planets around it. The great sidereal year covered by the sun in going through the twelve signs of the zodiac includes over 25,000 mortal years of 365 days each. While this immense circuit is being traversed, the sun drags the whole solar system with him around his own tremendous orbit, and we may imagine- for there are no observations on the point- that, while the 25,000 years of travel around the zodiac have been passing, the solar system as a whole has advanced along the sun's own orbit only a little distance.

But after millions of years shall have been consumed in these progresses, the sun must bring his train of planets to stellar space where they have never been before; here other conditions and combinations of matter may very well obtain- conditions and states of which our scientists have never heard, of which there never has been recorded one single phenomenon; and the difference between planetary conditions then and now will be so great that no resemblance shall be observed.

This is a branch of cyclic law with which the Eastern

sages are perfectly familiar. They have inquired into it, recorded their observations, and preserved them. Having watched the uncountable lives during cycles upon cycles past, and seen their behavior under different conditions in other stellar spaces long ago left behind, they have some basis upon which to draw conclusions as to what will be the state of things in ages yet to come. This brings us to an interesting theory offered by Theosophy respecting life itself as exhibited by man, his death and sleep. It relates also to what is generally called 'fatigue.' The most usual explanation for the phenomenon of sleep is that the body becomes tired and more or less depleted of its vitality and then seeks repose. This, says Theosophy, is just the opposite of the truth, for, instead of having suffered a loss of vitality, the body, at the conclusion of the day, has more life in it than when it waked.

During the waking state the life-waves rush into the body with greater intensity every hour, and, we being unable to resist them any longer than the period usually observed, they overpower us and we fall asleep. While sleeping, the life waves adjust themselves to the molecules of the body; and when the equilibrium is complete we again wake to continue the contest with life. If this periodical adjustment did not occur, the life current would destroy us. Any derangement of the body that tends to inhibit this adjustment is a cause of sleeplessness, and perhaps death. Finally, death of the body is due to the inequality of the contest with the life force- it at last overcomes us, and we are compelled to sink into the grave. Disease, the common property of the human race, only reduces the power of the body to adjust and resist. Children, say the Adepts, sleep more than adults, and need earlier repose, because the bodily machine, being young and tender, is easily overcome by life and made to sleep.

Of course, in so short an article, I cannot elaborate this

theory; but, although not probably acceptable now to Science, it will be one day accepted as true. As it is beginning to be thought that electricity is all-pervading, so, perhaps, ere long it will be agreed that life is universal even in what we are used to calling dead matter. As, however, it is plain to any observant mind that there seems to be more or less intelligence in the operations of this life energy, we naturally approach another interesting Theosophical doctrine as to the beings and hierarchies directing this energy.

VI

While studying these ancient ideas, we may as well prepare ourselves to have them clash with many long-accepted views. But since Science has very little save conjecture to offer when it attempts to solve the great problems of genesis and cosmogenesis, and, in the act of denying old dogmas, almost always starts with a hypothesis, the Theosophist may feel safe. In important matters, such as the heat of the sun or the history of the moon there is no agreement between scientists or astronomers. Newton, Pouillet, Zollner, Secchi, Fizcau, Waterston, Rosetti, and others all differ about the sun, the divergence between their estimates of its heat being as high as 8,998,600 degrees.

If we find the Adepts stating that the moon is not a mass thrown off from the earth in cooling, but, on the contrary, is the progenitor of this globe, we need not fear the jeers of a Science that is as uncertain and unsafe in many things as it is positive. Had I to deal only with those learned men of the schools who abide by the last utterance from the mouths of the leaders of Science, I should never attempt the task of speaking of the beings and hierarchies who guide the lives of which I wrote in my last. My pen would drop from a hand paralyzed by negations. But the spiritual beliefs of the common people will still be in vogue when the learned materialist has passed away. The great Immanuel Kant said:

"I confess I am much disposed to assert the existence of immaterial natures in the world, and to place my own soul in the class of these beings. It will hereafter, I know not where nor when, yet be proved that the human soul stands, even in this life, in indissoluble connection with all immaterial natures in the spirit world, that it reciprocally acts upon these, and receives impressions from them."

And the greater number of men think so also. That there are hierarchies ruling in the universe is not a new idea. It can be easily found today in the Christian Church. The early fathers taught it, St. Paul spoke of it, and the Roman Catholic Church has it clearly now in the Book of Ritual of the Spirits of the Stars. The four archangels who guard the four cardinal points represent the groups of rulers in the ancient system, or the heads of each group. In that system the rulers are named Dhyan Chohans. Although the Theosophical philosophy does not postulate a personal God, whether extra- or intra-cosmic, it cannot admit that Nature is left unaided in her work, but asserts that the Dhyan Chohans aid her, and are constantly occupied in directing- the all-pervading life in its evolutionary movement. Mme. Blavatsky, speaking on this subject in her 'Secret Doctrine' quotes from the old Book of Dzyan thus:

"An army of the Sons of Light stands at each angle, the Lipika in the middle wheel."

The four angels are the four quarters, and the 'middle wheel' is the center of space; and that center is everywhere, because as space is illimitable, the center of it must be wherever the cognizing consciousness is. And the same author, using the 'Disciple's Catechism' writes:

"What is it that ever is? Space, the Anupadaka.
What is it that ever was? The germ in the Root.
What is it that is ever coming and going? The great
Breath. Then there are three eternals? No, the three are
one. That which ever is is one; that which
ever was is one ; that which is ever being and becoming
is also one ; and this is space."

In this parentless and eternal space is the wheel in the center where the Lipika are, of whom I cannot speak; at the four angles are the Dhyan Chohans, and doing their will among men on this earth are the Adepts- the Mahatmas. The harmony of the spheres is the voice of the Law, and that voice is obeyed alike by the Dhyan Chohan and the Mahatma- on their part with willingness, because they are the law; on the part of men and creatures because they are bound by the adamantine chains of the law which they do not understand.

When I said that nothing could be spoken about the Lipika, I meant that, because of their mysterious nature and incomprehensible powers, it is not possible to know enough to say anything with either sense or certainty. But of the Dhyan Chohans and the Adepts we may know something, and are often given, as it were, tangible proof of their existence. For the Adepts are living men, using bodies similar to ours; they are scattered all over the earth in all nations; they know each other, but not according to mere forms and Masonic signs of recognition, unless we call natural, physical, and astral signs Masonic. They have times when they meet together and are presided over by some among their number who are more advanced in knowledge and power than the rest; and these higher Adepts again have their communications, at which that One who presides is the highest from these latter begins the communication with the Dhyan Chohans. All in their several degrees do that work which pertains to their degree, and although only to the Highest can be ascribed any governance or guidance of nature and mankind, yet the very least occupies an important place in the whole scheme. Freemasons and the numerous mock-Rosicrucians of the day will probably not unanimously accept this view, inasmuch as these Adepts have not submitted to their ritual; but that there has always been a widespread- and, if you please, a sometimes sneaking- belief in such beings and orders, is not difficult to discern or prove.

VII

An old argument for the existence of an extra-cosmic, a personal God, is this very intelligence that appears to pervade nature, from which the conclusion is drawn that there is a being who is the intelligent director. But Theosophy does not admit any such God, for he is neither necessary nor possible. There are too many evidences of implacability in the operations of nature for us to be able for very long to cherish the notion of a personal God. We see that storms will rage and overwhelm good and bad together; that earthquakes have no respect for age, sex or rank, and that wherever a natural law has to act it will do so regardless of human pain or despair.

The Wisdom Religion in postulating hierarchies such as those I have previously referred to, does not thereby outline a personal God. The difference between the personal God- say Jehovah for one- and the Lipika with the hosts of the Dhyan Chohans, is very great. Law and order, good sense, decency and progress are all subservient to Jehovah, sometimes disappearing altogether under his beneficent sway; while in the Wisdom Religion the Dhyan Chohans can only follow the immutable laws eternally traced in the Universal Mind, and this they do intelligently, because they are in fact men become gods. As these eternal laws are far-reaching, and as Nature herself is blind, the hierarchies- the hosts at the angles- have to guide the evolutionary progress of matter.

In order to grasp the doctrine better, let us take one period of manifestation such as that we are now in. This began millions of millions of years ago, succeeding a vast period of darkness or hibernation. It is called Chaos in the Christian scheme. And preceding that period of sleep there were eternally other periods of activity or manifestation. Now, in those prior periods of energy and action the same evolutionary progress went on, from and out of which came great beings- men perfected and become what to us are gods, who had aided in countless evolutions in the eternal past. These became Dhyan Chohans and took part in all succeeding evolutions. Such is the great goal for a human soul to strive after. Before it the paltry and impossible rewards of the Christian heaven turn to dross. The mistake must not be made of confining these great evolutionary periods and the beings spoken of, to our miserable earth. We are only in the chain. There are other systems, other spaces where energy, knowledge and power are exercised. In the mysterious Milky-Way there are spots vast in size and incomprehensibly distant, where there is room for many such systems as ours; and even while we now watch the assemblage of stars, there is some spot among them where the vast night of death is spreading remorselessly over a once fair system.

Now these beings, under the sway of the law as they are, seem perhaps to be sometimes implacable. Occasions are met where to mortal judgment it would seem to be wise or just to save a city from destruction, or a nation from decay, or a race from total extinction. But if such a fate is the natural result of actions performed or a necessary step in the cyclic sweep, it cannot be averted. As one of the Masters of this noble science has written: "We never pretended to be able to draw nations in the mass to this or that crisis in spite of the general drift of the worlds cosmic relations. The cycles must run their rounds.

Periods of mental and moral light and darkness succeed each other as day does night. The major and minor yugas must be accomplished according to the established order of things. And we, borne along on the mighty tide, can only modify and direct some of its minor currents. If we had the powers of the imaginary personal God, and the immutable laws were but toys to play with, then, indeed, might we have created conditions that would have turned this earth into an Arcadia for lofty souls."

And so in individual cases- even among those who are in direct relations with some Adept- the law cannot be infringed. Karma demands that such and such a thing should happen to the individual, and the greatest God or the smallest Adept cannot life a finger to prevent it. A nation may have heaped up against its account as a nation a vast amount of bad Karma. Its fate is sure, and although it may have noble units in it, great souls even who are Adepts themselves, nothing can save it, and it will 'go out like a torch dipped in water.'

Such was the end of ancient Egypt, of whose former glory no man of this day knows aught. Although to us she appears in the historical sky as a full-risen sun, she yet had her period of growth, when mighty Adepts sat upon the throne and guided the people. She gradually reached a high point of power and then her people grew material; the Adepts retired; pretended Adepts took their place, and gradually her glory weaned until at last the light of Egypt became darkness. The same story was repeated in Chaldea and Assyria and also upon the surface of our own America. Here a great, a glorious civilization once flourished, only to disappear as the others did; and that a grand development of civilization is beginning here again is one of the operations of the just and perfect law of Karma to the eye of the Theosophist, but one of the mysterious workings of an irresponsible providence to those who believe in a personal God who giveth the land of other men to the good Christian. The development of the American nation has a mysterious but potent connection with the wonderful past of the Atlanteans, and is one of those great stories outlined in the book of fate by the Lipika to whom I referred last week.

VIII

Among the Adepts the rise and fall of nations and civilizations are subjects which are studied under the great cyclic movements. They hold that there is an indissoluble connection between man and every event that takes place on this globe, not only the ordinary changes in politics and social life, but all the happenings in the mineral, vegetable and animal kingdoms. The changes in the seasons are for and through man; the great upheavals of continents, the movements of immense glaciers, the terrific eruptions of volcanoes, or the sudden overflowings of great rivers, are all for and through man, whether he be conscious of it or present or absent. And they tell of great changes in the inclination of the axis of the earth, past and to come, all due to man.

This doctrine is incomprehensible to the Western nineteenth century, for it is hidden from observation, opposed to tradition and contradicted by education. But the Theosophist who has passed beyond the elementary stages knows that it is true nevertheless. 'What,' says the worshiper of Science, 'has man got to do with the Charleston earthquake, or with the showers of cosmic dust that invade our atmosphere? Nothing.'

But the Adept, standing on the immeasurable height where centuries lie under his glance, sees the great cycles and the lesser ones rolling onward, influenced by man and working out their changes for his punishment, reward, experience and development. It is not necessary now to try to make it clear how the thoughts and deeds of men effect any changes in material things; that I will lay down for the present as a dogma, if you please, to be made clear later on.

The great subject of cycles has been touched upon, and brings us close to a most fascinating statement made by the Theosophical Adepts. It is this, that the cycles in their movement are bringing up to the surface now, in the United States and America generally, not only a great glory of civilization which was forgotten eleven thousand or more years ago, but also the very men, the monads- the egos, as they call them- who were concerned so many ages since in developing and bringing it to its final luster. In fact, we of the nineteenth century, hearing of new discoveries and inventions every day, and dreaming of great advances in all arts and sciences, are the same individuals who inhabited bodies among the powerful and brilliant as well as wicked, Atlanteans, whose name is forever set immortal in the Atlantic Ocean.

The Europeans are also Atlantean monads; but the flower, so to speak, of this revival or resurrection, is and is to be on the American continent. I will not say the United States, for mayhaps, when the sun of our power has risen again, there may be no United States for it to rise upon.

Of course, in order to be able to accept in any degree this theory, it is essential that one should believe in the twin Theosophical doctrines of Karma and Reincarnation, To me it seems quite plain. I can almost see the Atlanteans in these citizens of America, sleepy, and not well aware who they are, but yet full of the Atlantean ideas, which are only prevented from full and clear expression by the inherited bodily and mental environment which cramps and binds the mighty man within. This again is Nemesis-Karma that punishes us by means of these galling limitations, penning up our power and for the time frustrating our ambition. It is because, when we were in

ECHOES OF THE ORIENT

Atlantean bodies, we did wickedly, not the mere sordid wicked things of this day, but high deeds of evil such as by St. Paul were attributed to unknown spiritual beings in high places. We degraded spiritual things and turned mighty powers over nature to base uses; we did in excelsis that which is hinted at now in the glorification of wealth, of material goods, of the individual over the spiritual and above the great Man- Humanity. This has now its compensation in our present inability to attain what we want or to remove from among us the grinding-stones of poverty. We are, as yet, only preparers, much as we may exalt our plainly crude American development.

Herein lies the very gist of the cycle's meaning. It is a preparatory cycle with much of necessary destruction in it; for, before construction, we must have some disintegration. We are preparing here in America a new race which will exhibit the perfection of the glories that I said were being slowly brought to the surface from the long forgotten past. This is why the Americas are seen to be in a perpetual ferment. It is the seething and bubbling of the older races in the refining-pot, and the slow coming up of the material for the new race. Here, and nowhere else, are to be found men and women of every race living together, being governed together, attacking nature and the problems of life together, and bringing forth children who combine, each one, two races. This process will go on until in the course of many generations there will be produced on the American continents an entirely new race; new bodies, new orders of intellect, new powers of the mind, curious and unheard-of psychic powers, as well as extraordinary physical ones, with new senses and extensions of present senses now unforeseen.

When this new sort of body and mind are generated- then other monads, or our own again, will animate them and paint upon the screen of time the pictures of 100,000 years ago.

IX

In dealing with these doctrines one is compelled now and then to greatly extend the scope and meaning of many English words. The word 'race' is one of these. In the Theosophical scheme, as given out by the sages of the East, seven great races are spoken of. Each one of these includes all the different so called races of our modern ethnology. Hence the necessity for having seven great root-races, sub-races, family races, and countless offshoot races. The rootrace sends off sub-races, and these divide into family groups; all, however, being included in the great root-race then undergoing development. The appearance of these great root-races is always just when the world's development permits. When the globe was forming, the first root-race was more or less ethereal and had no such body as we now inhabit.

The cosmic environment became more dense and the second race appeared, soon after which the first wholly disappeared. Then the third came on the scene, after an immense lapse of time, during which the second had been developing the bodies needed for the third. At the coming of the fourth root-race it is said that the present human form was evolved, although gigantic and in some respects different from our own. It is from this point- the fourth race- that the Theosophical system begins to speak of man as such. The old book quoted by Mme. Blavatsky has it in this wise; 'Thus two by two on the seven zones the third race gave birth to the fourth;' and, 'The first race on every zone was moon-colored; the second, yellow, like gold; the third, red; the fourth, brown, which became black with sin.'

Topinard, in his 'Anthropology' gives support to this, as he says that there are three fundamental colors in the human organism- red, yellow and black. The brown race, which became black with sin, refers to the Atlantean sorcerer race of which I spoke in my last; its awfully evil practices, both mental and physical, having produced a change in the color of the skin.

The evolution of these seven great races covers many millions of years, and it must not be forgotten that when the new race is fully evolved the preceding race disappears, as the monads in it have been gradually reincarnated in the bodies of the new race. The present root-race to which we belong, no matter what the sub-race or family we may be in, is the fifth. It became a separate, distinct and completely-defined race about one million years ago, and has yet many more years to serve before the sixth will be ushered in. This fifth race includes also all the nations in Europe, as they together form a family race and are not to be divided off from each other.

Now, the process of forming the foundation, or great spinal column, for that race which is to usher in the sixth, and which I said is now going on in the Americas, is a slow process for us. Obliged as we are by our inability to judge or to count except by relativity, the gradual coming together of nations and the fusion of their offspring over and over again so as to bring forth something new in the human line, is so gradual as to seem almost without progress. But this change and evolution go on nevertheless, and a very careful observer can see evidences of it. One fact deserves attention. It is the inventive faculty displayed by Americans. This is not accorded much force by our scientists, but the Occultist sees in it an evidence that the brains of these inventors are more open to influences and pictures from the astral world than are the brains of the older nations. Reports have been brought to me by competent persons of children, boys and girls, who were born with most abnormal faculties of speech, or memory or otherwise, and some such cases I have seen myself. All of these occur in America, and many of them in the West. There is more nervousness here than in the older nations. This is accounted for by the hurry and rush of our civilization; but such an explanation really explains nothing, because the question yet remains, 'Why is there such hurry and push and change in the United States?' Such ordinary arguments go in a circle, since they leave out of sight the fundamental reason, so familiar to the Theosophist, that it is human evolution going on right before our eyes in accordance with cyclic laws.

The Theosophical Adepts believe in evolution, but not that sort which claims an ape as our ancestor. Their great and comprehensive system is quite able to account for rudimentary muscles and traces of organs found complete only in the animal kingdom without having to call a pithecoid ape our father, for they show the gradual process of building the temple for the use of the divine Ego, proceeding ceaselessly, and in silence, through ages upon ages, winding in and out among all the forms in nature in every kingdom, from the mineral up to the highest. This is the real explanation of the old Jewish, Masonic and archaic saying that the temple of the Lord is not made with hands and that no sound of building is heard in it.

X

It is well now to say, more definitely than I have as yet, a few words of the two classes of beings, one of which has been much spoken of in Theosophical literature, and also by those on the outside who write of the subject either in seriousness or in ridicule. These two classes of exalted personages are the Mahatmas and Nirmanakayas. In respect to the Mahatmas, a great many wrong notions have currency, not only with the public, but as well with Theosophists in all parts of the world. In the early days of the Theosophical Society the name Mahatma was not in use here, but the title then was 'Brothers.' This referred to the fact that they were a band of men who belonged to a brotherhood in the East. The most wonderful powers and, at times, the most extraordinary motives were attributed to them by those who believed in their existence. They could pass to all parts of the world in the twinkling of an eye. Across the great distance that India is from here they could precipitate letters to their friends and disciples in New York. Many thought that if this were done it was only for amusement; others looked at it in the light of a test for the faithful, while still others often supposed Mahatmas acted thus for pure love of exercising their power. The Spiritualists, some of whom believed that Mme. Blavatsky really did the wonderful things told of her, said that she was only a medium, pure and simple, and that her Brothers were familiar spooks of seance rooms. Meanwhile the press in general laughed, and Mme. Blavatsky and her Theosophical friends went on doing their work and never gave up their belief in the Brothers, who after a few years came to be called Mahatmas.

Indiscriminately with Mahatma the worthy Adept has been used to describe the same beings, so that we have these two titles made use of without accuracy and in a misleading fashion. The word Adept signifies proficiency, and is not uncommon, so that, when using it, some description is necessary if it is to be applied to the Brothers. For that reason I used Theosophical Adepts in a previous paper. A Mahatma is not only an Adept, but much more. The etymology of it will make the matter clearer, the word being strictly Sanskrit, from maha, great, and atma, soul-hence Great Soul. This does not mean a noble hearted man merely, but a perfected being, one who has attained to the state often described by mystics and held by scientific men to be an impossibility, when time and space are no obstacles to sight, to action, to knowledge or to consciousness. Hence they are said to be able to perform the extraordinary feats related by various persons, and also to possess information of a decidedly practical character concerning the laws of nature, including that mystery for science- the meaning, operation and constitution of life itself- and concerning the genesis of this planet as well as the races upon it. These large claims have given rise to the chief complaint brought forward against the Theosophical Adepts by those writers outside of the Society who have taken the subject up- that they remain, if they exist at all, in a state of cold and selfish quietude, seeing the misery and hearing the groans of the world, yet refusing to hold out a helping hand except to a favored few; possessing knowledge of scientific principles, or of medicinal preparations, and yet keeping it back from learned men or wealthy capitalists who desire to advance commerce while they turn an honest penny. Although, for one, I firmly believe, upon evidence given me, in all that is claimed for these Adepts, I declare groundless the complaint advanced, knowing it to be due to a want of knowledge of those who are impugned.

Adepts and Mahatmas are not a miraculous growth, nor the selfish successors of some who, accidentally stumbling upon great truths, transmitted them to adherents under patent rights. They are human beings trained, developed, cultivated through not only a life but long series of lives, always under evolutionary laws and quite in accord with what we see among men of the world or of science. Just as a Tyndall is greater than a savage, though still a man, so is the Mahatma, not ceasing to be human, still greater than a Tyndall. The Mahatma-Adept is a natural growth, and not produced by any miracle; the process by which he so becomes may be to us an unfamiliar one, but it is in the strict order of nature.

Some years ago a well-known Anglo-Indian, writing to the Theosophical Adepts, queried if they had ever made any mark upon the web of history, doubting that they had. The reply was that he had no bar at which to arraign them, and that they had written many an important line upon the page of human life, not only as reigning in visible shape, but down to the very latest dates when, as for many a long century before, they did their work behind the scenes. To be more explicit, these wonderful men have swayed the destiny of nations and are shaping events today. Pillars of peace and makers of war such as Bismarck, or saviors of nations such as Washington, Lincoln and Grant, owe their elevation, their singular power, and their astonishing grasp upon the right men for their purposes, not to trained intellect or long preparation in the schools of their day, but to these very unseen Adepts, who crave no honors, seek no publicity and claim no acknowledgment. Each one of these great human leaders whom I have mentioned had in his obscure years what he called premonitions of future greatness, or connection with stirring events in his native land. Lincoln always felt that in some way he was to be an instrument for some great work, and the stray utterances of Bismarck point to silent hours, never openly referred to, when he felt an impulse pushing him to whatever of good he may have done. A long array of instances could be brought forward to show that the Adepts have made 'an ineffaceable mark upon diverse eras.' Even during the great uprising in India that threatened the English rule there, they saw long in advance the influence England and India would have in the affairs of the world through the very psychic and metaphysical changes of today, and often hastened to communicate, by their own occult and wonderful methods, the news of successes for English arms to districts and peoples in the interior who might have risen under the stimulus of imaginary reports of English disasters. At other times, vague fears were spread instantly over large masses of the Hindus, so that England at last remained master, even though many a patriotic native desired another result. But the Adepts do not work for the praise of men, for the ephemeral influence of a day, but for the future races and man's best and highest good.

XI

For an exhaustive disquisition upon Adepts, Mahatmas and Nirmanakayas, more than a volume would be needed. The development illustrated by them is so strange to modern minds and so extraordinary in these days of general mediocrity, that the average reader fails to grasp with ease the views advanced in a condensed article; and nearly everything one would say about Adepts- to say nothing of the Nirmanakayas- requiring full explanation of recondite laws and abstruse questions, is liable to be misunderstood, even if volumes should be written upon them.

The development, conditions, powers, and function of these beings carry with them the whole scheme of evolution; for, as said by the mystics, the Mahatma is the efflorescence of an age. The Adepts may be dimly understood to-day, the Nirmanakayas have as yet been only passingly mentioned, and the Mahatmas are misconceived by believers and deniers alike.

But one law governing them is easy to state and ought not to be difficult for the understanding. They do not, will not, and must not interfere with Karma; that is, however apparently deserving of help an individual may be, they will not extend it in the manner desired if his Karma does not permit it; and they would not step into the field of human thought for the purpose of bewildering humanity by an exercise of power which on all sides would be looked upon as miraculous. Some have said that if the Theosophical Adepts were to perform a few of their feats before the eyes of Europe, an immense following for them would at once arise; but such would not be the result. Instead of it there would be dogmatism and idolatry worse than have ever been, with a reaction of an injurious nature impossible to counteract.

Hypnotism- though by another name- has long been known to them. The hypnotic condition has often aided the schemes of priests and churches. To compel recognition of true doctrine is not the way of these sages, for compulsion is hypnotism. To feed a multitude with only five loaves would be easy for them; but as they never act upon sentiment but continually under the great cosmic laws, they do not advance with present material aid for the poor in their hands. But, by using- their natural powers, they every day influence the world, not only among the rich and poor of Europe and America, but in every other land, so that what does come about in our lives is better than it would have been had they not had part therein.

The other class referred to- Nirmanakayas- constantly engage in this work deemed by them greater than earthly enterprises; the betterment of the soul of man, and any other good that they can accomplish through human agents. Around them the long-disputed question of Nirvana revolves, for all that they have not been distinctly considered in it. For, if Max Muller's view of Nirvana, that it is annihilation, be correct, than a Nirmanakaya is an impossibility. Paradoxically speaking, they are in and out of that state at one and the same time. They are owners of Nirvana who refuse to accept it in order that they may help the suffering orphan. Humanity.

They have followed the injunction of the Book of the Golden Precepts: "Step out from sunlight into shade, to make more room for others."

A greater part is taken in the history of nations by the Nirmanakayas than anyone supposes. Some of them have under their care certain men in every nation who from their birth are destined to be great factors in the future. These they guide and guard until the appointed time. And such proteges but seldom know that such influence is about them, especially in the nineteenth century. Acknowledgment and appreciation of such great assistance are not required by the Nirmankayas, who work behind the veil and prepare the material for a definite end. At the same time, too, one Nirmanakaya may have many different men- or women- whom he directs. As Patanjali puts it, "In all these bodies one mind is the moving cause."

ECHOES OF THE ORIENT

Strange, too, as it may seem, often such men as Napoleon Bonaparte are from time to time helped by them. Such a being as Napoleon could not come upon the scene fortuitously. His birth and strange powers must be in the order of nature. The far reaching consequences going with a nature like his, immeasurable by us, must in the eastern Theosophical philosophy be watched and provided for. If he was a wicked man, so much the worse for him; but that could never deter a Nirmanakaya from turning him to his uses. That might be by swerving him, perchance, from a path that would have plunged the world into depths of woe and been made to bring about results in after years which Napoleon never dreamed of. The fear of what the world might think of encouraging a monster at a certain point never can deter a sage who sees the end that is best. And in the life of Napoleon there are many things going to show at times an influence more powerful than he could grapple. His foolhardy march to Moscow was perhaps engineered by these silent campaigners, and also his sudden and disastrous retreat.

What he could have done had he remained in France, no present historian is competent to say. The oft-doubted story of the red letter from the Red Man just when Napoleon was in a hesitating mood, may have been an encouragement at a particular juncture. "Whom the gods would destroy, they first make mad." Nor will the defeat at Waterloo be ever understood until the Nirmanakayas give their records up.

As a change in the thought of a people who have been tending to gross atheism is one always desired by the Sages of the Wisdom Religion, it may be supposed that the wave of spiritualistic phenomena resulting now quite clearly in a tendency back to a universal acknowledgment of the soul, has been aided by the Nirmanakayas. They are in it and of it; they push on the progress of a psychic deluge over great masses of people. The result is seen in the literature, the religion and the drama of today. Slowly but surely the tide creeps up and covers the once dry shore of Materialism, and, though priests may howl, demanding 'the suppression of Theosophy with a firm hand,' and a venal press may try to help them, they have neither the power nor the knowledge to produce one backward ripple, for the Master hand is guided by omniscient intelligence propelled by a gigantic force, and works behind the scene.

XII

There have been so many secret societies during the Christian era, by whom claims were made to knowledge of nature's secret laws, that a natural question arises: 'In what do the Theosophic Eastern Sages differ from the many Rosicrucians and others so often heard of?' The old bookshelves of Germany are full of publications upon Rosicrucianism, or by pretended and genuine members of that order, and to-day it is not uncommon to find those who have temerity enough to dub themselves 'Rosicrucians.'

The difference is that which exists between reality and illusion, between mere ritualism and the signs printed by nature upon all things and beings passing forever up the road to higher states of existence. The Rosicrucian and Masonic fraternities known to history rely upon outward signs and tokens to indicate the status in the order of their members, who, without such guarantees, are only uninitiated outsiders.

But the Sages we speak of, and their disciples, carry with them the indelible mark and speak the well-known words that show they are beings developed under laws, and not merely persons who, having undergone a childish ordeal, are possessed of a diploma. The Adepts may be called rugged oaks that have no disguise, while the undeveloped man dabbling in Masonic words and formulas is only a donkey wearing a lion's skin. There are many Adepts living in the world, all of whom know each other. They have means of communication unknown to modern civilization, by using which they can transmit to and receive from each other messages at any moment and from immense distances, without using any mechanical means. We might say that there is a Society of Adepts, provided that we never attach to the word 'society' the meaning ordinarily conveyed by it. It is a society which has no place of meeting, which exacts no dues, which has no constitution or by-laws other than the eternal laws of nature; there are no police or spies attached to it and no complaints are made or received in it, for the reason that any offender is punished by the operation of law entirely beyond his control- his mastery over the law being lost upon his infringing it.

Under the protection and assistance and guidance of this Society of Adepts are the disciples of each one of its members. These disciples are divided into different degrees, corresponding to the various stages of development; the least developed disciples are assisted by those who are in advance of them, and the latter in a similar manner by others, until the grade of disciple is reached where direct intercourse with the Adepts is possible. At the same time, each Adept keeps a supervisory eye upon all his disciples.

Through the agency of the disciples of Adepts many effects are brought about in human thought and affairs, for from the higher grades are often sent those who, without disclosing their connection with mysticism, influence individuals who are known to be main factors in events about to occur. It is claimed that the Theosophical Society receives assistance in its growth and the spreading of its influence from the Adepts and their accepted disciples. The history of the Society would seem to prove this, for unless there were some hidden but powerful force operating for its advantage it would have long ago sunk into obscurity, destroyed by the storm of ridicule and abuse to which it has been subjected. Promises were made, in the early history of the Society, that assistance would at all times be rendered, and prophecies were hinted that it would be made the target for vilification and the object of opposition. Both prophecies have been fulfilled to the letter. In just the same way as a polished diamond shows the work which gives it value and brilliancy, so the man who has gone through probation and teaching under the Adepts carries upon his person the ineffaceable marks. To the ordinary eye untrained in this department, no such indications are visible; but those who can see describe them as being quite prominent and wholly beyond the control of the bearer. For this reason that one who has progressed, say, three steps along the way, will have three marks, and it is useless to pretend that his rank is a step higher, for, if it were, then the fourth mark would be there, since it grows with the being's development. Now, as these signatures cannot be imitated or forged, the whole inner fraternity has no need for concealment of signs. No one can commit a fraud upon or extract from them the secrets of higher degrees by having obtained signs and pass-words out of a book or in return for the payment of fees, and none can procure the conferring of any advancement until the whole nature of the man exactly corresponds to the desired point of development.

In two ways the difference between the Adept fraternity and the worldly secret societies can be seen in their treatment of nations and of their own direct special disciples. Nothing is forced or depends upon favor. Everything is arranged in accordance with the best interests of a nation, having in view the cyclic influences at any time prevailing, and never before the proper time. When they desire to destroy the chains forged by dogmatism, they do not make the error of suddenly appearing before the astonished eyes of the people; for they know well that such a course would only alter the dogmatic belief in one set of ideas to a senseless and equally dogmatic adherence to the

Adepts as gods, or else create in I the minds of many the surety that the devil was present.

XIII

The training of the disciple by the teachers of the school to which the Theosophical Adepts belong is peculiar to itself, and not in accord with prevailing modern educational ideas. In one respect it is a specialization of the pilgrimage to a sacred place so common in India, and the enshrined object of the journey is the soul itself, for with them the existence of soul is one of the first principles. In the East the life of man is held to be a pilgrimage, not only from the cradle to the grave, but also through that vast period of time, embracing millions upon millions of years, stretching from the beginning to the end of a Manvantara, or period of evolution, and as he is held to be a spiritual being, the continuity of his existence is unbroken. Nations and civilizations rise, grow old, decline and disappear; but the being lives on, spectator of all the innumerable changes of environment. Starting from the great All, radiating like a spark from the central fire, he gathers experience in all ages, under all rulers, civilizations and customs, ever engaged in a pilgrimage to the shrine from which he came. He is now the ruler and now the slave; today at the pinnacle of wealth and power, to-morrow at the bottom of the ladder, perhaps in abject misery, but ever the same being. To symbolize this, the whole of India is dotted with sacred shrines, to which pilgrimages are made, and it is the wish of all men in that so-called benighted land to make such a journey at least once before death, for the religious duties of life are not fully performed without visiting such sacred places.

One great reason for this, given by those who understand the inner significance of it, is that the places of pilgrimage are centers of spiritual force from which radiate elevating influences not perceptible to the pig-sticking, wine-drinking traveler. It is asserted by many, indeed, that at most of the famous places of pilgrimage there is an Adept of the same order to which the Theosophical Adepts are said to belong, who is ready always to give some meed of spiritual insight and assistance to those of pure heart who may go there. He, of course, does not reveal himself to the knowledge of the people, because it is quite unnecessary, and might create the necessity for his going elsewhere. Superstitions have arisen from the doctrine of pilgrimages, but, as that is quite likely to come about in this age, it is no reason why places of pilgrimage should be abolished, since, if the spiritual centers were withdrawn, good men who are free from superstition would not receive the benefits they now may have. The Adepts founded these places in order to keep alive in the minds of the people the soul idea which modern Science and education would soon turn into agnosticism, were they to prevail unchecked.

But the disciple of the Adept knows that the place of pilgrimage symbolizes his own nature, shows him how he is to start on the scientific investigation of it and how to proceed, by what roads and in which direction. He is supposed to concentrate into a few lives the experience and practice which it takes ordinary men countless incarnations to acquire. His first steps, as well as his last, are on difficult, often dangerous places; the road, indeed, 'winds up hill all the way,' and upon entering it he leaves behind the hope for reward so common in all undertakings.

Nothing is gained by favor, but all depends upon his actual merit. As the end to be reached is self-dependence with perfect calmness and clearness, he is from the beginning made to stand alone, and this is for most of us a difficult thing which frequently brings on a kind of despair. Men like companionship, and cannot with ease contemplate the possibility of being left altogether to themselves. So, instead of being constantly in the company of a lodge of fellow-apprentices, as is the case in the usual worldly secret society, he is forced to see that, as he entered the world alone, he must learn to live there in the same way, leaving it is he came, solely in his own company. But this produces no selfishness, because, being accompanied by constant meditation upon the unseen, the knowledge is acquired that the loneliness felt is only in respect to the lower, personal, worldly self.

Another rule this disciple must follow is that no boasting may be indulged in on any occasion, and this gives us the formula that, given a man who speaks of his powers as an Adept or boasts of his progress on the spiritual planes, we can be always sure he is neither Adept nor disciple. There have been those in the Theosophical Society who gave out to the world that they were either Adepts in fact or very near it, and possessed of great powers. Under our formula it follows that they were mere boasters, with nothing behind their silly pretensions but vanity and a fair knowledge of the weakness as well as the gullibility of human nature; upon the latter they play for either their profit or pleasure. But, hiding themselves under an exterior which does not attract attention, there are many of the real disciples in the world. They are studying themselves and other human hearts. They have no diplomas, but there resides in them a consciousness of constant help and a clear knowledge of the true Lodge which meets in real secrecy and is never found mentioned in any directory. Their whole life is a persistent pursuit of the fast-moving soul which, although appearing to stand still, can distance the lightning; and their death is only another step forward to greater knowledge through better physical bodies in new lives.

XIV

Looking back into the past the nineteenth-century historian finds his sight speedily striking a mist and at last plunging into inky darkness. Bound down in fact by the influence of a ridiculous dogmatism which allows only some six thousand years for man's life on earth, he is unwilling to accept the old chronologies of the Egyptians or Hindus, and, while permitting the assumption of vast periods for geological changes, he is staggered by a few millions of years more or less when they are added to the length of time during which humanity has peopled the globe. The student of Theosophy, however, sees no reason why he should doubt the statement made by his teachers on this subject. He knows that the periods of evolution are endless. These are called Manvantaras, because they are between two Manus, or, two men. These periods may be called waves whose succession has no cessation. Each grand period, including within it all the minor evolutions, covers 311,040,000,000,000 human years; under a single Manu the human years come and go, 306,720,000 in number, and the lesser yugas- or ages- more immediately concerning us, comprise of solar years 4,320,000.

During these solar revolutions the human races sweep round and round this planet. Cave-dwellers, lake dwellers and those of a neolithic or any other age appear and disappear over and over again, and in each of those we who now read, write and think of them were ourselves the very Egos whose past we are trying to trace. But, going deep into geological strata, the doubt of man's existence contemporaneously with the plesiosaurus arises because no fossil genus homo is discovered in the same stratum. It is here that the theories of the Theosophist come in and furnish the key. Those hold that before man developed any physical body he clothed himself with an astral form; and this is why H. P. Blavatsky writes in her Secret Doctrifie; 'it teaches the birth of the astral before the physical body, the former being the model for the latter.' At the time of the huge antediluvian animals they absorbed in their enormous bodies so much of the total quantity of gross matter available for frames of sentient beings that the astral man remained without a corporeal frame, as yet unclothed 'with coats of skin.' For this reason he could exist in the same place with those huge birds and reptiles without fear. Their massive proportions inspired him with no terror, and by their consumption of food there was no lessening of his sustenance. And, therefore, being of such a composition that he left no impression upon mud or plastic rock, the death of one astral body after another left no fossil and no mark to be unearthed by us in company with the very beasts and birds which were his contemporaries.

Man was all this time acquiring the power to clothe himself with a dense frame. He threw off astral bodies one after another, in the ceaseless pursuit, each effort giving him a little more density. Then he began to cast a shadow, as it were, and the vast, unwieldy animal world- and others as well- felt more and more the draughts made upon it by the coming man. As he thickened they grew smaller, and his remains could not be deposited in any stratum until such time as he had grown to sufficient hardness. But our modern anthropologists have not yet discovered when that was. They are ready enough to make definite statements, but, learned as they are, there are surprises awaiting them not so far off.

While, therefore, our explorers are finding, now and then, the remains of animals and birds and reptiles in strata which show an age far greater than any assigned to the human race, they never come upon human skeletons. How could man leave any trace at a stage when he could not press himself into the clay or be caught by soft lava or masses of volcanic dust? I do not mean, however, to say that the period of the plesiosaurus is the period of the man of astral body devoid of a material one. The question of exact period may well be left for a more detailed account; this is only to point to the law and to the explanation for the non-appearance of man's remains in very early geologic strata. But the Theosophic Adepts insist that there are still in the earth bony remains of man, which carry his first appearance in a dense body many millions of years farther back than have yet been admitted, and these remains will be discovered by us before much time shall have rolled away.

One of the first results of these discoveries will be to completely upset the theory as to the succession of ages, as I may call it, which is given and accepted at the present time, and also the estimation of the various civilizations that have passed from the earth and left no trace except in the inner constitution of ourselves- for it is held that we are those very persons now in different bodies, who so long ago lived and loved and died upon the planet. We began to make Karma then and have been under its influence ever since, and it seems fitting that that great doctrine should be taken up at another time for a more careful examination.

XV

The Oriental doctrine of reward and punishment of the human Ego is very different from the theological scheme accepted throughout Christendom, since the Brahmins and Buddhists fix the place of punishment and compensation upon this earth of ours, while the Christian removes the 'bar of God' to the hereafter. We may not profitably stop to argue upon logic with the latter; it will be sufficient to quote to them the words of Jesus, St. Matthew, and the Psalmist. "With what measure ye mete, it shall be measured unto you again," said Jesus; and Matthew declares that for every word, act, and thought we shall have to answer, while David, the royal poet, sang that those who serve the Lord should never eat beggar's bread. We all know well that the first two declarations do away with the vicarious atonement; and as for the Jewish singer's notion, it is negatived every day in any city of either hemisphere.

ECHOES OF THE ORIENT

Among the Ceylonese Buddhists the name of the doctrine is Kamma; with the Hindus it is Karma. Viewed in its religious light, it "is the good and bad deeds of sentient beings, by the infallible influence or efficacy of which those beings are met with due rewards or punishment, according as they deserve, in any state of being." (The Rev. T P. Terunnanse, High-Priest at Dodanduwa, Ceylon.) When a being dies, he emits, as it were, a mass of force or energy, which goes to make up the new personality when he shall be reincarnated. In this energy is found the summation of the life just given up, and by means of it the Ego is forced to assume that sort of body among those appropriate circumstances which together are the means for carrying out the decrees of. Karma.

Hence hell is not a mythical place or condition after death in some unknown region specially set apart by the Almighty for the punishment of his children, but is in very truth our own globe, for it is on the earth, in earth-lives experienced in human bodies, that we are punished for bad deeds previously done, and meet with happiness and pleasure as rewards for old merit. When one sees, as is so common, a good man suffering much in his life, the question naturally arises, 'Has Karma anything to do with it, and is it just that such a person should be so afflicted?' For those who believe in Karma it is quite just, because this man in a previous life must have done such acts as deserve punishment now. And, similarly, the wicked man who is free from suffering, happy and prosperous, is so because in a previous existence he had been badly treated by his fellows or had experienced much suffering. And the perfect justice of Karma is well illustrated in his case because, although now favored by fortune, he, being wicked, is generating causes which, when he shall be reborn, will operate then to punish him for his evil-doing now.

Some may suppose that the Ego should be punished after

death, but such a conclusion is not logical. For evil deeds committed here on the objective plane could not with any scientific or moral propriety be published on a plane which is purely subjective. And such is the reason why so many minds, both of the young and old, have rejected and rebelled against the doctrine of a hellfire in which they would be eternally punished for commission of sin on earth. Even when unable to formulate the reason in metaphysical terms, they instinctively knew that it would be impossible to remove the scene of compensation from the very place where the sin and confusion had been done and created. When the disciples of Jesus asked him if the man who was born blind was thus brought into the world for some sin he had committed they had in mind this doctrine of Karma, just as all the Hindus and Buddhists have when they see some of their fellows crippled or deformed or deprived of sight.

The theory above hinted at of the person at death throwing out from himself the new personality, so to speak, ready to await the time when the Ego should return to earth seeking a new body, is a general law that operates in a great many other instances besides the birth or death of a being. It is that which is used by the Theosophists to explain the relations between the moon and the earth. For, as the moon is held by them to be the planet on which we lived before reaching the earth and before there was any such earth whatever; and that, when our so-called satellite came to die, all the energy contained in it was thrown out into space, where in a single vortex it remained until the time came for that energy to be again supplied with a body- this earth- so the same law prevails with men, the single units in the vast aggregate which is known among advanced Theosophists as the great Manu. Men being, as to their material envelope, derived from the moon, must follow the law of their origin, and therefore the Buddhist priest says, as quoted: 'At the death of a being nothing goes out from him to the other world for his rebirth; but by the efficacy- or, to use a more

46

figurative expression, by the ray- of influence which Kamma emits, a new being is produced in the other world very identical with the one who died away, for in this 'new being' is held all the life of the deceased. The term 'being,' as applied to it may be taken by us with some qualification. It is more properly a mass of energy devoid of conscience and crowded with desires of the person from whom it emanated; and its special province is to await the return of the individuality and form for that the new body in which it shall suffer or enjoy. Each man is therefore his own creator under the great Cosmic laws that control all creations. A better term in place of 'creation' is 'evolution,' for we, from life to life, are engaged in evolving out of the material provided in this Manvantara new bodies at every turn of the wheel of rebirth. The instruments we use in this work are desire and will. Desire causes the will to fix itself on objective life; in that plane it produces force and out of that comes matter in its objective form.

XVI

Very many Western people say that this Oriental doctrine of Karma is difficult to understand, being fit only for educated and thoughtful persons. But in India, Ceylon and Burma, not to mention other Asiatic countries, the whole mass of the people accept and seem to understand it. The reason for this lies probably in the fact that they also firmly believe in Reincarnation, which may be said to be the twin doctrine to Karma. Indeed, the one cannot be properly considered without keeping the other in view, for Karma- whether as punishment or reward- could have no actual or just operation upon the Ego unless the means for its operation were furnished by Reincarnation.

Our deserts are meted out to us while we are associating in life with each other, and not while We are alone, nor in separateness. If being raised to power in a nation or becoming possessed of wealth is called a reward, it would lose all value were there no people to govern and no associated human beings with and upon whom we could spend our wealth and who might aid us in satisfying our manifold desires. And so the law of Reincarnation drags us into life again and again, bringing with us uncounted times the various Egos whom we have known in prior births. This is in order that the Karma- or causes- generated in company with those Egos may be worked out, for to take us off separately into an unknown hell, there to receive some sort of punishment, or into an impossible serio-comic heaven to meet our reward, would be as impossible as unjust. Hence, no just hanged murderer absolved by priest or praising Jesus can escape.

He, together with his victim, must return to this earth, each to aid the other in adjusting the disturbed harmony, during which process each makes due compensation. With this doctrine we restore justice to her seat in the governance of men, for without it the legal killing of the murderer after condemnation is only a half remedy, since no provision is made by the State for the being hurled out of the body nor for the dependents he may have left behind, and, still further, nothing is done for those who in the family of the murderer survive him. But the Theosophical sages of all ages push the doctrine of Karma beyond a mere operation upon incarnated men. They view all worlds as being bound together and swayed by Karma. As the old Hindu book, the Bhagavad- Gita, says, "all worlds up to that of Brahma are subject to Karma." Hence it acts on all planes. So viewing it, they say that this world as it is now conditioned is the actual result of what it came to be at the beginning of the pralaya or grand death which took place billions upon billions of years ago. That is, the world evolves just as man does. It is born, it grows old, it dies, and it is reincarnated.

This goes on many times, and during those incarnations

it suffers and enjoys in its own way for its previous evolutions. For it the reward is a greater advance along the line of evolution, and the punishment is a degraded state. Of course, as I said in a former article, these states have man for their object and cause, for he is the crown of all evolution. And, coming down from the high consideration of great cosmic spaces and phenomena, the Theosophist is taught to apply these laws of Karma and Reincarnation to every atom in the body in especial and apart from the total Karma. Since we are made up of a mass of lives, our thoughts and acts affect those atoms or lives and impress them with a Karma of their own. As the Oriental thinkers say, "not a moment passes without some beings coming to life in us, acquiring Karma, dying, and being reincarnated."

The principal divisions of Karma are three in number. One sort is that now operating in the present life and body, bringing about all the circumstances and changes of life. Of this we see illustrations every day, with now and then strange climaxes which throw upon the doctrine the brightest light. One such is immortalized in India by a building erected by the favored son of fortune, as we would say, and thus it came about. A Rajah had a very strange dream, so affecting that he called upon his soothsayers for interpretation. They said that their horoscopes showed he was required next day to give an immense sum of money to the first person he should see after awaking, their intention being to present themselves at an early hour. Next day the King arose unusually early, stepped to his window, threw it open, and there before him was a chandalah sweeping up the dirt. To him he gave a fortune, and thus in a moment raised him to affluence from abject poverty.

The chandalah then built a huge building to commemorate his sudden release from the grinding chains of poverty. Another class of Karma is that which is held over and not now in operation because the man does not furnish the appropriate means for bringing it into action. This may be likened to vapor held in suspension in the atmosphere and not visible to the eye, but which will fall as rain upon the earth the moment conditions are ripe. The last chief class is that Karma which we are making now, and which will be felt by us in future births. Its appropriate symbol is the arrow shot forward in the air by the archer.

XVII

The Spirit is not affected by Karma at any time or under any circumstances, and so the Theosophical Adepts would not use the terms 'cultivation of the Spirit.' The Spirit in man, called by them Ishwara is immutable, eternal and indivisible- the fundamental basis of all. Hence they say that the body and all objects are impermanent and thus deluding to the soul whenever they are mistaken for reality.

They are only real on and for this plane and during the time when the consciousness takes them up here for cognition. They are therefore relatively real and not so in an absolute sense. This can easily be proved from dreams. In the dream state we lose all knowledge of the objects which while awake we thought real and proceed to suffer and enjoy in that new state. In this we find the consciousness applying itself to objects partaking of course of the nature of the experiences of the waking condition, but at the same time producing the sensations of pleasure and pain while they last. Let us imagine a person's body plunged in a lethargy extending over twenty years and the mind undergoing a pleasant or unpleasant dream, and we have a life just of that sort, altogether different from the life of one awake. For the consciousness of this dreamer the reality of objects known during the waking state is destroyed.

But as material existence is a necessary evil and the one

in which alone emancipation or salvation can be obtained, it is of the greatest importance and hence Karma which governs it and through whose decrees emancipation may be reached must be well understood and then be accepted and obeyed. Karma will operate to produce a deformed or deficient body, to give in a good body a bad disposition or vice versa; it will cause diseases, hurts or annoyances, or bring about pleasures and favorable situations for the material frame. So we sometimes find with a deformed or disagreeable body a most enlightened and noble mind. In this case the physical Karma is bad and the mental good.

This leads us to the sort of Karma that works upon the mental plane. At the same time that an unfavorable Karmic cause is showing forth in the physical structure another and better sort is working out in the mind and disposition or has eventuated in conferring a mind well balanced, calm, cheerful, deep, and brilliant. Hence we discover a purely physical as compared with an entirely mental Karma. Purely physical would be that resulting, say from a removal from the ground of fruit peel which might otherwise cause some unknown person to fall and be hurt. Purely mental might be due to a life spent in calm, philosophical thought and the like. There is in one of the Hindu books a strange sentence respecting this part of the subject, reading: "Perfection of body or superhuman powers are produced by birth or by herbs or by incantations, penances, or meditations."

Among mental afflictions esteemed as worse than any bodily hurt or loss is that Karma from a preceding life which results in obscurity of such a character that there is a loss of all power to conceive of the reality of Spirit or the existence of soul- that is, materialism. The last field of operation for this law may be said to be the psychical nature. Of this in America we have numerous examples in mediums, clairvoyants, clairaudients, mind-readers, hysterics, and all sorts of abnormal sensitives. There could be no clairvoyant according to the Oriental scheme if the person so afflicted, using as I think the proper term, had not devoted much of previous lives to a one-sided development of the psychical nature resulting now in powers which make the possessor an abnormality in society.

A very strange belief of the Hindus is that one which allows the possibility of a change of state by a mortal of such a character that the once man becomes a Deva or lesser god. They divide nature into several departments, in each of which are conscious powers or entities called Devas, to put it roughly. Yet this is not so far apart from the ideas of some of our best scientific men who have said there is no reason why in each ray of the spectrum there may not be beings to us unseen. Many centuries ago the Hindu thinker admitted this, and pushing further on declared that a man might through a certain sort of Karma become one of these beings, with corresponding enjoyment and freedom from care, but with the certainty, however, of eventually changing back again to begin the weary round of birth over again.

What might be called the doctrine of the nullification of Karma is an application in this department of the well-known law in physics which causes an equilibrium when two equal forces oppose each other. A man may have in his Karmic account a very unpleasant cause and at the same time a cause of opposite character. If these come together for expression at the same time they may so counteract each other as that neither will be apparent and the equilibrium is the equivalent of both. In this way it is easy to understand the Biblical verse: 'Charity covereth a multitude of sins,' as referring to the palliative effect of charitable deeds as opposed to deeds of wickedness, and giving a reason for the medieval knight devoting some of the years of his life to alms giving.

ECHOES OF THE ORIENT

In the Bhagavad-Gita, a book revered by all in India, the highest place is given to what is called Karma- Yoga or the Religion of the Performance of Works and Duty, and there it is said: "He who, unattached to the fruits of his actions, performs such actions as must be done, is both renouncer and devotee; not he who kindles no sacrificial fires and performs no ceremonies. He who remains inert, restraining the organs of action, and pondering with his heart on objects of sense, is called a false pietist of bewildered soul. But he who, restraining his senses by his heart and being free from interest in acting, undertakes active devotion through the organs of action, is praiseworthy."

XVIII

That the doctrine of Karma is unjust, unsympathetic, and fatalistic has been claimed by those who oppose it, but such conclusions are not borne out by experience among those races who believe in it, nor will the objections stand a close examination. The Hindus and Buddhists thoroughly believe in Karma, convinced that no one but themselves punishes or rewards in this or any life, yet we do not find them cold or unsympathetic. Indeed, in the relations of life it is well known that the Hindu is as loving and tender as his American brother, and there are as many instances of heroic self-sacrifice in their history as in ours. Some go further than this and say that the belief in Karma and Reincarnation has made the Hindu more gentle in his treatment of men and animals than are the Europeans, and more spiritual in his daily life. Going deeper into their history, the belief in Karma is found side by side with material works of great magnitude, and whose remains to this day challenge our wonder, admiration, and respect; it is doubtful whether we could ever show such triumphs over nature as can be seen at any time in the rock-cut temples of Hindustan. So it would appear that this doctrine of ours is not likely to produce bad or enervating effects upon the people who accept it.

'But,' says an objector, 'it is fatalism. If Karma is Karma, if I am to be punished in such and such a manner, then it will come about so whether I will or not, and hence I must, like the Turk, say 'Kismet,' and do nothing.' Now, although the Mohammedan doctrine of Kismet has been abused as fatalism, pure and simple, it was not so held by the Prophet nor by his greatest disciples, for they taught that it was law and not fate. And neither is Karma amenable to this objection. In the minds of those who, having vaguely apprehended Karma as applying to one life only, do not give the doctrine its true majestic, endless sweep, fatalism is the verdict. When, on the other hand, each man is seen as the fashioner of the fate for his next fleeting earth personality, there can be no fatality in it, because in his own hand is the decree. He set in motion the causes which will inevitably have certain results. Just as easily he could have made different causes and thus brought about different results.

That there are a repellent coldness and want of tenderness in a doctrine which thus deals out inflexible justice and compels us to forever lose our friends and beloved relatives, once death has closed the door, is the feeling of a few who make sentiment their rule in life. But while sentiment and our own wishes are not the guiding laws of nature, there is no reason even on the sentimental ground for this objection; it is due to a partial knowledge of the doctrine which, when fully known, is found to be as full of opportunity for the exercise of what is dear to the heart as any other theory of life. The .same law that throws us into life to suffer or enjoy, as may be deserved, decrees that the friends and the relatives who are like unto each other must incarnate together, until by reason of differentiation of character they cannot under any law of attraction remain in company. Not unless and until they become different do they separate from each other. And who would wish to be eternally tied to the side of uncongenial relatives or acquaintances merely because there was an accident of birth! For our aid also this law works well and ceaselessly.

"Those whom you help will help you in other lives," is the declaration. In ages past perhaps we knew those who long since have passed up to greater heights. The very moment in the long series of incarnations we come near to where they are pursuing their pilgrimage, they at once extend assistance, whether that be on the material or moral planes. And it makes no difference whether one or the other is aware of who is assisting or who is being assisted. Inflexible law guides the current and brings about the result. Thus the members of the whole human family reciprocally act on one another, forced into it by a law which is as kind as it is great, which turns the contempt we bore in the past into present honor and opportunity to help our fellows.

There is no favoritism possible in nature; no man has any privilege or gift which he has not deserved, either as a reward or a compensation. Looking at the present life spread before our limited vision, we may see perhaps no cause why there should be any such reward to an unworthy man, but Karma never errs and will surely repay. And it not only rewards, but to it solely belong those compensations which we with revenge attempt to mete out. It is with this in view that the holy writ of the Christians says, 'Vengeance is mine; I will repay,' for so surely as one hurts another so is the certainty of Karma striking the offender- but let the injured one beware that he does not desire the other punished, for by Karma will he be punished also. So from all this web of life and ceaselessly revolving- wheel, Karma furnishes the escape and the means of escape, and by reincarnation we are given the time for escape.

XIX

In the Egyptian Book of the Dead, chapter 10 describes

'the place where, after death, disembodied souls remain in different degrees of perfection. Some are shown as taking wheat three cubits high, while others are only permitted to glean it- he gleaned the fields of Aanroo.' Thus some enjoy the perfection of spiritual bliss, while others attain only to minor degrees in that place or state where divine justice is meted out to the soul.

Devachan is the land of reward; the domain of spiritual effects. The word spiritual here refers to disembodiment; it must only be used as relative to our material existence. The Christian demonstrates this fact by the material entourage of his heaven. In the Secret Doctrine, H. P. Blavatsky says: "Death itself is unable to deliver man from it (Karma), since death is simply the door through which he passes to another life on earth, after a little rest on its threshold- Devachan." Devachan, then, is the threshold of life. In the Hindu system it is etymologically the place of the gods, Indra's heaven. Indra is the regent of heaven, who gives to those who can reach his realm long-enduring gifts of happiness and dominion.

The Bhagavad Gita says: 'After enjoying felicity for innumerable years in the regions of Indra, he is born again upon this earth.'

For the purpose of this article, we assume that the entire man, minus the body, goes into Devachan. This, however, is not so. The post-mortem division of our seven-fold constitution given by Theosophy is exact. It exhibits the basis of life, death and reincarnation. It shows the composite being, man, in analogy with that other composite being, nature. Both are a unity in diversity. Man, suspended in nature, like her, divides and retinites. This seven-fold division will be treated in a future article. Devachan, being a state of prolonged subjective happiness after the death of the body, is plainly the heaven of the Christian, but with a difference. It is a heaven made scientifically possible. Heaven itself must accord with the divine laws projected into nature. As sleep is a release from the body, during which we have dreams, so death is a complete separation and release, after which in Devachan we dream; until, on being again incarnated in a new body on earth, we come once more into what we call waking existence. Even the human soul would weary of the ceaseless round of rebirths, if some place or state were not provided in which rest could be obtained; in which germinating aspirations, restricted by earth life, could have their full development. No energy can be annihilated, least of all a psychic energy; these must somewhere find an outlet. It is found in Devachan; this realization is the rest of the soul.

Its deepest desires, its highest needs are there enjoyed. There every hope blooms out in full and glorious flower. To prolong 'this blissful state, Hindu books give many incantations and provide innumerable ceremonies and sacrifices, all of them having for end and aim a long stay in Devachan. The Christian does precisely the same. He longs for heaven, prays that he may go there, and offers up to his God such propitiatory rites and acts as seem best to him, the only difference being that he does not do it half so scientifically as the Hindu. The Hindu is also more vivid in his conception of this heaven than the Christian is. He postulates many places or conditions adapted to the energetic and qualitative differences between souls. Kama-loka and other states are where concrete desires, restricted by life in the body, have full expression, while in Tribuvana the abstract and benevolent thinkers absorb the joys of lofty thought. The orthodox heaven has no such proviso. It also ignores the fact that a settled monotony of celestial existence would exhaust the soul-would be stagnation, not growth. Devachanic life is development of aspiration, passing through the various stages of gestation, birth, cumulative growth, downward momentum and departure to another condition, all rooted in joy. There is nothing in the mere fact of death to mold a soul anew. It is a group of psychic energies, and heaven must have something in common with these, or why should it gravitate there? Souls differ as men do. In Devachan each one receives that degree of bliss which it can assimilate; its own development determines its reward. The Christian places all the snuffy old saints as high as other holy souls, sinking genius to the level of the mediocre mass, while the Hindu gives infinite variety of occupation and existence suited to grave and gay, the soul of genius or of poetry. No one sits in undesired seats, nor sings psalms he never liked, nor lives in a city which might pall upon him if he were forever compelled to walk its pearly streets. The laws of cause and effect forbid that Devachan should be monotonous. Results are proportionate to antecedent energies. The soul oscillates between Devachan and earth-life, finding in each conditions suited to its continuous development, until, through effort, it reaches a perfection in which it ceases to be the subject of the laws of action and reaction, becoming instead their conscious coworker.

Devachan is a dream, but only in the sense in which objective life can be called such. Both last until Karma is satisfied in one direction, and begins to work in the other. The Devachanee has no idea of space or time except such as he makes for himself. He creates his own world. He is with all he ever loved, not in bodily companionship, but in one to him real, close and blissful. When a man dies, the brain dies last. Life is still busy there after death has been announced. The soul marshals up all past events, grasps the sum total, the average tendency stands out, the ruling hope is seen. Their final aroma forms the keynote of Devachanic existence. The lukewarm man goes neither to heaven nor hell. Nature spews him out of her mouth. Positive conditions, objective or subjective, are only reached through positive impulsion. Devachanic distribution is governed by the ruling motive of the soul. The hater may, by reaction, become the lover, but the indifferent have no propulsion, no growth.

ECHOES OF THE ORIENT

XX

It is quite evident to the unprejudiced inquirer that Christian priests for some reason or other studiously ignore the composite nature of man, although their great authority, St. Paul, clearly refers to it. He spoke of body, soul, and spirit, they only preach of body and soul; he declared we had a spiritual body, they remain misty as to the soul's body and cling to an absurd resurrection of the material casket. It became the duty of Theosophists to draw the attention of the modern mind once more to the Oriental division of man's constitution, for through that alone can an understanding of his state before and after death be attained. The division laid down by St. Paul is threefold, the Hindu one is of a seven-fold character. St. Paul's is meant for those who require broad outlines, but do not care to inquire into details.

Spirit, soul, and body, however, include the whole seven divisions, the latter being a more complete analysis; and it is suspected by many deep thinkers that Paul knew the complete system but kept it back for good reasons of his own. An analysis of body discloses more than mere molecular structure, for it shows a force or life or power that keeps it together and active throughout its natural period. Mr. Sinnett, in his "Esoteric Buddhism" attempting to bring to his countrymen some knowledge of the Eastern system, called this Prana or Jiva; others, however, call it Prana alone, which seems more appropriate, because the human aspect of the life force is dependent upon Prana, or breath.

The spirit of St. Paul may be taken for our purposes to be the Sanskrit Atma. Spirit is universal, indivisible, and common to all. In other words, there are not many spirits, one for each man, but solely one spirit which shines upon all men alike, finding as

59

many souls- roughly speaking- as there are beings in the world. In man the spirit has a more complete instrument or assemblage of tools with which to work. This spiritual identity is the basis of the philosophy; upon it the whole structure rests; to individualize spirit, assigning to each human being his own spirit, particular to him and separate from the spirit of any other man, is to throw to the ground the whole Theosophic philosophy, will nullify its ethics and defeat its object. Starting, then, with Atma- spirit- as including the whole, being its basis and support, we find the Hindu offering the theory of sheaths or covers of the soul or inner man. These sheaths are necessary the moment evolution begins and visible objects appear, so that the aim of the soul may be attained in conjunction with nature. In this way, through a process which would be out of place here, a classification is arrived at by means of which the phenomena of life and consciousness may be explained.

The six vehicles (adopting Mr. Sinnett's nomenclature) used by the spirit and by means of which the Ego gains experience are:

> Body, as a gross vehicle.
> Vitality, or Prana.
> Astral Body, or Linga Carira.
> Animal Soul, or Kama Rupa.
> Human Soul, or Manas.
> Spiritual Soul, or Buddhi.

The Linga Carira is needed as a more subtle body than the corporeal frame, because the latter is in fact only stupid, inert matter. Kama Rupa is the body, or collection, of desires and passions; Manas may be properly called the mind, and Buddhi is the highest intellection beyond brain or mind. It is that which discriminates. At the death of the body, Prana flies back to the reservoir of force; the astral body dissipates after a longer period and often returns with Kama Rupa when aided by certain other forces to seance-rooms, where it masquerades as the deceased, a continual lie and ever-present snare. The human and the spiritual soul go into the state spoken of before as Devachan or heaven, where the stay is prolonged or short according to the energies appropriate to that state generated during earth-life. When these begin to exhaust themselves the Ego is gradually drawn back to earth-life, where through human generation it takes up a new body, with another astral body, vitality, and animal soul.

This is the 'wheel of rebirth,' from which no man can escape unless he conforms to true ethics and acquires true knowledge and consciousness while living in a body. It was to stop this ceaselessly revolving wheel that Buddha declared his perfect law, and it is the aim of the true Theosophist to turn his great and brilliant 'Wheel of the Law' for the healing of the nations.

XXI

High in the esteem of the Hindu stands the serpent, both as a symbol and a creature. Moving in a wavy line, he figures the vast revolution of the Sun through eternal space carrying the rapidly whirling Earth in her lesser orbit; periodically casting his skin, he presents a visible illustration of renewal of life or reincarnation; coiling to strike, he shows the working of the law of Karma-Nemesis which, with a basis in our actions, deals an unerring blow. As a symbol with tail in mouth, forming a circle, he represents eternity, the circle of necessity, all-devouring Time. For the older Initiates he spoke to them also of the astral light which is at once devilish and divine. Probably in the whole field of Theosophic study there is nothing so interesting as the astral light. Among the Hindus it is known as Akasa, which can also be translated as aether. Through a knowledge of its properties they say that all the wonderful phenomena of the Oriental Yogis are accomplished. It is also claimed that clairvoyance, clairaudience, mediumship, and seership as known to the Western world are possible only through its means. It is the register of our deeds and thoughts, the great picture gallery of the earth, where the seer can always gaze upon any event that has ever happened, as well as those to come. Swimming in it as in a sea are beings of various orders and also the astral remains of deceased men and women. The Rosicrucians and other European mystics called these beings Sylphs, Salamanders, Gnomes, Undines, Elementals; the Hindu calls them Gandharbhas or celestial musicians, Yakshas, Rakshasas and many more. The 'spooks' of the dead- mistaken by Spiritualists for the individuals who are no more- float in this Akasic substance, and for centuries have been known to the mystical Hindu as Bhuta, another name for devil, or Pisacha, a most horrible devil; neither of them any more than the cast-off soul-body nearest earth, devoid of conscience and only powerful for evil.

But the term 'astral light,' while not new, is purely of Occidental origin. Porphyry spoke of it when referring to the celestial or soul-body, which he says is immortal, luminous, and 'star-like;' Paracelsus called it the 'sidereal light;' later it grew to be known as astral. It was said to be the same as the anima mundi or soul of the world. Modern scientific investigators approach it when they speak of 'luminiferous ether' and 'radiant matter.' The great astronomer, Camille Flammarion, who was a member of the Theosophical Society during his life, speaks on the astral light in his novel Urania and says: "The light emanating from all these suns that people immensity, the light reflected through space by all these worlds lighted by these suns, photographs throughout the boundless heaven the centuries, the days, the moments as they pass... From this it results that the histories of all the worlds are traveling through space without dispersing altogether, and that all the events of the past are present and live evermore in the bosom of the infinite."

Like all unfamiliar or occult things the astral light is difficult to define, and especially so from the very fact that it is called 'light.' It is not the light as we know it, and neither is it darkness. Perhaps it was said to be a light because when clairvoyants saw by means of it, the distant objects seemed to be illuminated. But as equally well distant sounds can be heard in it, heavy bodies levitated by it, odors carried thousands of miles through it, thoughts read in it, and all the various phenomena by mediums brought about under its action, there has been a use of the term 'light' which while unavoidable is none the less erroneous. A definition to be accurate must include all the functions and powers of this light, but as those are not fully known even to the mystic, and wholly terra incognita for the scientist, we must be content with a partial analysis. It is a substance easily imagined as imponderable ether which, emanating from the stars, envelopes the earth and permeates every atom of the globe and each molecule upon it. Obeying the laws of attraction and repulsion, it vibrates to and fro, making itself now positive and now negative. This gives it a circular motion which is symbolized by the serpent. It is the great final agent, or prime mover, cosmically speaking, which not only makes the plant grow but also keeps up the diastole and systole of the human heart.

Very like the action of the sensitive photographic plate is this light. It takes, as Flammarion says, the pictures of every moment and holds them in its grasp. For this reason the Egyptians knew it as the Recorder; it is the Recording Angel of the Christian, and in one aspect it is Yama, the judge of the dead in the Hindu pantheon, for it is by the pictures we impress therein that we are judged by Karma. As an enormous screen or reflector the astral light hangs over the earth and becomes a powerful universal hypnotizer of human beings. The pictures of all acts good and bad done by our ancestors as by ourselves, being ever present to our inner selves, we constantly are impressed by them by way of suggestion and go then and do likewise. Upon this the great French priest-mystic, Eliphas Levi, says: "We are often astonished when in society at being assailed by evil thoughts and suggestions that we would not have imagined possible, and we are not aware that we owe them solely to the presence of some morbid neighbor; this fact is of great importance, since it relates to the manifestation of conscience- one of the most terrible and incontestable secrets of the magic art... So diseased souls have a bad breath, and vitiate the moral atmosphere; that is to say, they mingle impure reflections with the astral light which penetrates them, and thus establish deleterious currents." (Dogma et Ritual de Haute Magic)

There is also a useful function of this light. As it preserves the pictures of all past events and things, and as there is nothing new under the sun, the appliances, the ideas, the philosophy, the arts and sciences of long buried civilizations are continually being projected in pictures out of the astral into the brains of living men. This gives a meaning not only to the oft-recurring 'coincidence' of two or more inventors or scientists hitting upon the same ideas or inventions at about the same time and independently of each other, but also to other events and curious happenings.

Some self-styled scientists have spoken learnedly of telepathy, and other phenomena, but give no sufficient reason in nature for thought-transference or apparitions or clairvoyance or the hundred and one varieties of occurrences of an occult character noticed from day to day among all conditions of men. It is well to admit that thought may be transferred without speech directly from one brain to another, but how can the transference be effected without a medium? That medium is the astral light.

ECHOES OF THE ORIENT

The moment the thought takes shape in the brain it is pictured in this light, and from there is taken out again by any other brain sensitive enough to receive it intact. Knowing the strange properties of the astral plane and the actual fate of the sheaths of the soul spoken of in another article, the Theosophical Adepts of all times gave no credit to pretended returning of the dead. Eliphas Levi learned this well and said: "The astral light combining with ethereal fluids forms the astral phantom of which Paracelsus speaks. This astral body being freed at death, attracts to itself and preserves for a long time, by the sympathy of likeness, the reflection of the past life; if a powerfully sympathetic will draws it into the proper current it manifests itself in the form of an apparition."

But with a sensitive, abnormally constituted person present- a medium, in other words, and all of that class are nervously unbalanced- the strong will is not needed, for the astral light and the living medium's astral body recall these soulless phantoms, and out of the same reservoir take their speech, their tones, their idiosyncrasies of character, which the deluded devotees of this debasing practice are cheated into imagining as the returned self of dead friend or relative. Yet all I have referred to here are only instances of a few of the various properties of the astral light. So far as concerns our world it may be said that astral light is everywhere, interpenetrating all things; to have a photographic power by which it grasps pictures of thoughts, deeds, events, tones, sounds, colors, and all things, reflective in the sense that it reflects itself into the minds of men; repellent from its positive side and attractive from the negative; capable of assuming extreme density when drawn in around the body by powerful will or by abnormal bodily states, so that no physical force can penetrate it. This phase of its action explains some facts officially recorded during the witchcraft excitement in Salem. It was there found that although stones and other flying objects came toward the possessed one they always fell as it were from the force of gravity just at the person s feet. The Hindu Yogi gives evidence of a use of this condensation of the astral light when he allows arrows and other projectiles to be thrown at him, all of them falling at his feet no matter how great their momentum, and the records of genuine Spiritualistic phenomena in the United States furnish similar experiences.

The astral light is a powerful factor, unrecognized by science, in the phenomenon of hypnotism. Its action will explain many of the problems raised by Binet, Charcot and others, and especially that class in which two or more distinct personalities seem to be assumed by the subject, who can remember in each only those things and peculiarities of expression which belong to that particular stratum of their experience. These strange things are due to the currents in the astral light. In each current will be found a definite series of reflections, and they are taken up by the inner man, who reports them through speech and action on this plane as if they were his own. By the use of these currents too, but unconsciously, the clairvoyants and clairaudients seem to read in the hidden pages of life.

This light can therefore be impressed with evil or good pictures, and these are reflected into the subconscious mind of every human being. If you fill the astral light with bad pictures, just such as the present century is adept at creating, it will be our devil and destroyer, but if by the example of even a few good men and women a new and purer sort of events are limned upon this eternal canvas, it will become our Divine Uplifter.

THE THEOSOPHICAL SOCIETY

HOW TO JOIN IT

This Society is not a secret or political organization. was founded in New York in November, 1875. Its objects are:

First: To form a nucleus of a Universal Brotherhood of Humanity, without distinction of race, creed, or color.

Second: To promote the study of Aryan and other Eastern literatures, religions, and sciences, and demonstrate the importance of that study.

Third: To investigate unexplained laws of nature and the psychical powers latent in man.

The Society appeals for support and encouragement to all who truly love their fellow-men and desire the eradication of the evils caused by the barriers raised by race, creed, or color, which have so long impeded human progress; to all scholars, to all sincere lovers of truth, wheresoever it may be found and to all philosophers, alike in the East and in the West; and lastly, to all who aspire to higher and better things than the mere pleasures and interests of a worldly life, and are prepared to make the sacrifices by which alone a knowledge of them can be attained. The Headquarters are at Adyar, a suburb of Madras, India, where the Society has a property of twenty-seven acres and extensive buildings, including one for the Oriental Library and a spacious hall wherein the General Council meets annually in Convention, on the 27th of December.

The Society is composed of its Branches and members, and is divided into four Sections: India, Ceylon, Europe, and

America. Each Section is autonomous and governs the Branches in its jurisdiction without interference from Headquarters, provided only that the fundamental rules of the Society are not violated. All Branches in America and the West Indies are under the jurisdiction of the American Section; these are all under the jurisdiction of the General Convention held in India.

The President of the Society is Col. H. S. Olcott, in India; the Corresponding Secretary is H. P. Blavatsky, London; the Vice-President, William Q. Judge, New York.

Throughout the world there are about 180 Branches. The American Section includes at this date the 42 Branches in the United States, in the principal cities. Members are either Branch members or members at large, the latter being those who are not in Branches. The Annual Convention of the American, Section is held on the fourth Sunday of April. At each Convention an Executive Committee is elected, and during the year administers the affairs of the Section under the Constitution and Laws passed in Convention. This Committee for 1889-90 is: Gen. Abner Doubleday, Mendham, N. J. ; Dr. J. D. Buck, 124 W. 7th St., Cincinnati, Ohio; Alexander Fullerton, Box 2659, New York, N. Y. ; E. A. Neresheimer, 21 Maiden Lane, New York; Dr. J. W. B. LaPierre, Box 71, Minneapolis, Minn.; Arthur B. Griggs, Young's Hotel, Boston, Mass. ; William Q. Judge (General Secretary), Box 2659, New York, N. Y, The Society's literature is extensive and varied.

There are three magazines in English: The Theosophisty Adyar, Madras, India; monthly, $5.00 a year.

Lucifer 7 Duke St., London, W. C, England; $4.25 a year.

The Path, 132 Nassau St., New York, N.Y. ; $2.00 a year.

Other periodicals are in Asiatic and other languages. A circulating library of Theosophical books has been established in New York by private subscription, information as to which can be obtained by addressing "Theosophical Library, Box 2659, New York P. O."

HOW TO JOIN

Applicants become members by entering a Branch or by being admitted as 'at large.' In each case an application has to be signed and endorsed by two active members in good standing. Branch Presidents, as well as Councilors, the Executive Committee, and the General Secretary, have the right to admit members at large. Applications to enter a Branch must be made to the Branch officers. Any member-at-large can affiliate with a Branch by which he is accepted and those in Branches may sever that connection if they see fit and be admitted as 'at-large.' Entrance fee for members-at-large is $2,00, the annual dues $1.00, and the diploma fee 50 cents. Branches charge their own dues in addition. All members receive the yearly Report, such documents as are from time to time issued from the General Secretary's office, and a copy of The Forum, an occasional pamphlet containing questions and answers upon Theosophical topics, and which it is intended to issue monthly as near as may be. They are also entitled to the use (under the rules) of the Circulating Theosophical Library established at the Headquarters, Room 25, 132 Nassau St., New York. Additions to this Library are published in The Path.

Inquirers and applicants are requested to address the General Secretary at the address given below, enclosing a stamp, and will receive receive from him further information or application blanks.

William Q. Judge,
Gen. Secy American Section
P. O. Box 2659,
New York City.

(It should be noted that this and all other addresses herein are now outdated. -Editor.)

THE END

33342696R00039

Made in the USA
Lexington, KY
10 March 2019